THE NAKED MARRIAGE

———

DISCUSSION GUIDE

INTRODUCTION

Thank you for investing into your marriage! We believe that this journey you're about to undertake will bring more intimacy into every aspect of your relationship. We're excited for you to get started and we're honored to be part of your journey.

We pray that this experience will bring more "nakedness" to your relationship. When we refer to nakedness throughout the book and accompanying teaching videos, we're pointing back to God's original, perfect design for marriage outlined in Genesis chapter 2. The first couple was "naked and unashamed." Their nakedness wasn't just physical (although that part is definitely a fun and important aspect of marriage). They were naked spiritually, emotionally and physically. Their nakedness was a beautiful, God-given picture of total transparency, acceptance, honesty, vulnerability and intimacy. That's still God's design for marriage and that type of complete "naked" intimacy is possible for you and your spouse.

The Naked Marriage book, teaching videos and discussion guide will help you and your spouse grow deeper in your love for each other and your love for God as you work toward the total intimacy of *The Naked Marriage*. This experience will prompt conversations between you and your spouse that peel back layers of past hurts and help you move forward toward a new season of health and healing in your relationship. Even if your marriage is already rock-solid, we believe this experience can help you grow even stronger together!

If you're doing this experience within a Small Group, we encourage you to prioritize attendance and to be active in group discussions to help everyone involved get the most out of the experience. Your perspectives and experiences can help other couples, so don't be afraid to share. Speak up and get naked (please reserve physical nakedness for the privacy of your own home). Whether you're participating in the discussions within a small group setting or alone as a couple, please give your best energies to this experience and we believe it will bring many positive returns to your marriage.

As you go through these videos and discussions, please feel free to email us with your feedback. We'd love to hear from you! You can also get a weekly dose of encouragement by listening to us on *The Naked Marriage Podcast (available on Apple, Spotify & Google)*. We are praying for you and cheering you on!

Your friends,

Dave and Ashley

DaveWillis@MarriageToday.com | AshleyWillis@MarriageToday.com

HOW TO USE THIS DISCUSSION GUIDE

1. **The Discussion Guide** Read through each session together as a couple or with your group. The verses and key thoughts are great take-aways to meditate on.

2. **Watch the XO Now Online Videos** Dave & Ashley Willis provide a short time of teaching for each session. Watch the video that corresponds with your session.

3. **Questions & Activation** Work through some of the questions with your spouse and/or group. Then set aside a time to do the "Just Between Us" part together as a couple.

HOW TO WATCH THE XO NOW ONLINE VIDEOS

1. This discussion guide comes with **One Free Month of XO Now!** Go to xomarriage.com/now and enter the coupon code: NAKEDISGOOD during checkout.

2. Log into your XO Now account and search "Naked Marriage" to find *The Naked Marriage* videos.

*If you already have an XO Now account you can still use the Free Month off coupon by going to xomarriage.com/now/myaccount, clicking Edit Subscription, then Apply coupon, entering the coupon code and clicking update subscription. The discount will be applied to your next invoice.

**This coupon only works if you sign up through our website. It will not work if you try to sign up through the apps (Apple, Google, Roku, Amazon) or if you have previously signed up through the apps.

CONTENTS

NAKED IS GOOD

"Now the man and his wife were both naked,
but they felt no shame."

GENESIS 2:25 (NLT)

In the *naked marriage*, everything changes for the better. But before that can happen, there must be a commitment to vulnerability and *nakedness* in every way. Without real vulnerability and honesty, there can be no real love.

God wants to create a generational impact through your marriage. The level at which your marriage will make an eternal impact is defined by your level of commitment to pursuing and possessing a *naked marriage*. There is no relationship more sacred than your marriage, so treasure your spouse. Never let anyone or anything take the place of priority your spouse should hold in your heart. Marriage is one of God's greatest gifts.

"Make a commitment to transform your marriage. Stop taking each other for granted. Your best days together can still be ahead of you and not behind you." – Ashley Willis, The Naked Marriage | Pg. 10

THE STRONGEST
MARRIAGES ARE BUILT
ON A FOUNDATION OF
LOVE, VULNERABILITY,
AND COMMITMENT.

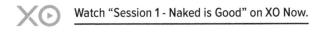

XO Watch "Session 1 - Naked is Good" on XO Now.

DISCUSSION QUESTIONS

1. Growing up, how did your parents influence your view of sex and love?

2. How did your parents influence your views of trust and vulnerability in marriage?

3. What does *The Naked Marriage* mean to you?

4. How would your marriage benefit from more vulnerability?

5. Ashley says, "We say, 'I do' every day to our spouse." What do you think she means by this? What would saying, "I do" to your spouse every day look like in your marriage?

6. How would your marriage be different if it was a naked marriage? Would anything need to change?

JUST BETWEEN US

Go for a walk and take turns sharing with each other one area in your marriage where you can be more vulnerable (*more naked*) in your relationship.

NAKED COMMUNICATION

"Instead, we will speak the truth in love,
growing in every way more and more like Christ,
who is the head of his body, the church."

EPHESIANS 4:15 (NLT)

Many of us stop effectively using our words when we marry. We make assumptions that our spouse gets us, so we don't need to honestly communicate with them anymore. If this starts happening, communication breaks down and the vulnerability and intimacy in our marriage begins to crumble.

If you struggle with communication, you are not alone! Talk with words to one another. Remove distractions when it comes to effective communication with your spouse.

God made us to crave connection and nothing replaces face to face conversation. Give your spouse your best attention.

When we make communication a priority, every other aspect of our marriage will begin to improve!

"Daily heart-to-heart conversation is the cornerstone of true intimacy."
– Dave Willis, The Naked Marriage | Pg. 18

BROKEN
RELATIONSHIPS
CAN BE HEALED
AND STRONG
MARRIAGES CAN
GROW STRONGER
THROUGH HONEST
COMMUNICATION.

XO ▶ Watch "Session 2 - Naked Communication" on XO Now.

DISCUSSION QUESTIONS

1. Why is it important to work on your communication daily?

2. What are words/phrases you say that shutdown communication between you and your spouse?

3. What are some ways that you can make time to have focused conversations with your spouse?

4. What is your non-verbal communication saying? What does your spouse say it is saying?

5. What is one example of an assumption that might cause conflict in your marriage?

6. How has the tone of your words affected your relationship with your spouse?

JUST BETWEEN US

Take time every day (even just 5 minutes), look into your spouse's eyes, and ask them one of these questions: "How are you doing? How was your day? Is there anything that you're worried about right now? What are you excited about right now?" Then listen to what they say.

NAKED FIGHTS

If it is possible, as far as it depends on you,
live at peace with everyone.

ROMANS 12:18 (NIV)

How we handle hardships, especially hardships we bring into the marriage, determines the level of nakedness in our marriage. Marriage requires an unshakable commitment to one another even when your spouse is intimately aware of your flaws.

When we are going through a tough season (and we all will at some point), we must resist the urge to face it alone. Leaning on each other during these difficult times is what will help you get through them while also keeping your marriage strong.

Allow love to lead your marriage, and you will always overcome any hardships that you face.

"When God created the concept of marriage, He simultaneously gave us an extraordinary gift and an extraordinary challenge." – Dave Willis, The Naked Marriage | Pg. 44

HARD TIMES ARE WHEN
YOU NEED EACH OTHER
THE MOST, AND IT'S
ESSENTIAL TO KNOW HOW
TO BRING PEACE TO ANY
MARRIAGE CONFLICT.

Watch "Session 3 - Naked Fights" on XO Now.

DISCUSSION QUESTIONS

1. How can mentors help your marriage?

2. When seeking marriage mentors, what should you be looking for?

3. Why is it important to never vent to your parents about your spouse or your marriage?

4. What are some things you can do if your communication on a touchy topic always results in an argument?

5. How does compromise happen in your marriage? Do both of you give respect and consideration to the other's perspective?

6. Give your ideas on how a couple can pursue peace together.

JUST BETWEEN US

Talk about an unresolved issue that is routinely a point of conflict between you and your spouse. Work through a compromise that will bring peace to your marriage.

Think about who might be a good marriage mentor for you and your spouse. What do you admire about them? Ask them out to dinner and find out what their "secret" is.

SESSION FOUR

NAKED SEX

The husband should fulfill his marital duty to his wife, and likewise the wife to her husband. The wife does not have authority over her own body but yields it to her husband. In the same way, the husband does not have authority over his own body but yields it to his wife.

1 CORINTHIANS 7:3-4 (NIV)

Sexual intimacy can and *should* be one of the most fulfilling and *fun* aspects of marriage, but it won't happen automatically.

Every couple must deal with issues in the bedroom. Baggage, expectations, hangups, hurts, and a myriad of other factors need to be communicated for both of you to experience physical pleasure, emotional intimacy, and the spiritual-oneness that God intends to happen whenever a husband and wife make love.

Sex is a gift from God that is exclusively for married couples, and we should do our very best to cultivate a thriving sex life with our spouse by talking openly and honestly about it with them and by having it often.

"Our marriages are strong when we choose to passionately pursue and affirm one another and when sex is a priority." – Ashley Willis, The Naked Marriage | Pg. 48

COUPLES THAT HAVE
THE BEST SEX LIVES
HAVE A MAN WHO
CONTINUOUSLY PURSUES,
ROMANCES, AND ADORES
HIS WIFE AND A WIFE
WHO CONTINUOUSLY
AFFIRMS HER HUSBAND
AND SHOWS HER RESPECT
AND BELIEF IN HIM.

DISCUSSION QUESTIONS

1. How did your upbringing affect your view of sexual intimacy? How did your peers and what was considered socially acceptable affect your view of sex?

2. What safeguards do you have in place to protect your marriage from pornography and other temptations that would taint the intimacy of your marriage?

3. How does learning that sex is God's idea and that He considers it a married couples' right and privilege affect your view of sex?

4. If you put your spouse's needs ahead of your own needs, how would your sex life be better? Do you think your marriage would benefit from more sex?

5. What would happen if you and your spouse had conversations about sex? Would it be uncomfortable for you? Or helpful? Explain.

6. How does sharing secrets from your past, or current struggles, strengthen your marriage? What are the things that stop you from sharing?

JUST BETWEEN US

Light a candle, put on some romantic music and get naked!

Talk about how you can make sexual intimacy and fulfillment a high priority in your marriage. Discuss together when the best times during the week for sex are and what distractions may be keeping you from sex.

Take turns talking about some things in each of your lives that may get in the way: past baggage or mistakes, porn, insecurities, busyness, exhaustion, medical issues, etc. There may need to be some counseling involved to work through these issues.

NAKED HONESTY

"Do not lie to each other, since you have taken off your old self with its practices and have put on the new self, which is being renewed in knowledge in the image of its Creator."

COLOSSIANS 3:9-10 (NIV)

Secrecy ruins relationships. It is often the very reason why a relationship ends. Secrecy clouds our judgment and erodes honesty, trust, and intimacy in our marriages.

Honesty heals relationships. It makes us feel secure, sets a positive course for our lives, and chases away our fears in the process.

Naked honesty in marriage means having nothing to hide from each other. It means full transparency. It means giving your spouse an all-access key to your heart, your mind, your hopes, your fears, and every other part of your life.

"In marriage, any form of secrecy is really an act of infidelity. When we value our own privacy at the expense of the sacred vows we made to our spouse, we're chipping away at the foundation of trust that every strong marriage must be built upon." – Dave Willis, The Naked Marriage | Pg. 81

HONESTY HAS THE POWER
TO SET A POSITIVE COURSE
FOR YOUR LIFE AND
MARRIAGE, WHILE ALSO
CHASING AWAY YOUR FEARS
IN THE PROCESS; TRUE
INTIMACY STARTS WITH
NAKED HONESTY.

Watch "Session 5 - Naked Honesty" on XO Now.

DISCUSSION QUESTIONS

1. What stops you from being completely honest with your spouse?

2. Why is confession so hard? What is your biggest fear about confessing a struggle?

3. Does it make you trust your spouse more or less when they have been honest with you?

4. What does speaking the truth in love look like?

5. How do you make yourself a safe place for your spouse?

6. How is secrecy the enemy of intimacy?

7. What is an example of basing our honesty on God's truth rather than our feelings?

JUST BETWEEN US

Is there something in your life that needs to be confessed to God and to your spouse? Sit down in a safe place and talk about it together. It doesn't have to be something significant to be something that is stopping you from enjoying *naked*, honest intimacy. If you're the one listening, communicate that you are a safe place for your spouse.

SESSION SIX

NAKED SCARS

The Spirit of the Sovereign LORD is on me, because the
LORD has anointed me to proclaim good news to the
poor. He has sent me to bind up the brokenhearted,
to proclaim freedom for the captives and release from
darkness for the prisoners.

ISAIAH 61:1 (NIV)

Marriage is a choice, a lifelong commitment, not a lifelong sentence. It requires vulnerability, and when we feel like we've been in an exposed position and then experience pain, shame, or rejection, our defense mechanisms can actually work against us sabotaging our marriages.

We can also unintentionally create new wounds from past pain if we are not focused on healing from the past and moving forward in a healthy way.

In marriage, we are one. It's not his or her problem, it's our problem. When we lean on God and one another, there is nothing we can't get through.

"None of us are immune to pain from the past, and all of us can benefit
from healing. The health of your present and future relationships may
hinge on how you choose to address the issue of healing from your
past." – Ashley Willis, The Naked Marriage | Pg. 97

GOD WANTS TO HEAL
YOU SO YOU CAN
EXPERIENCE A LOVING
MARRIAGE IN ITS
FULLNESS.

Watch "Session 6 - Naked Scars" on XO Now.

DISCUSSION QUESTIONS

1. What benefit does the healing from past scars have on your present relationship?

2. How do you usually respond when your spouse unintentionally touches the areas of your heart where you are already hurting (your emotional sunburn)?

3. What can we do to heal and to help our spouse heal from past hurts? How can you be a support for your spouse when they are struggling and need healing from hurt?

4. What is your default communication style? Does it make things better or worse?

5. What are other forms of communication we can use when how we normally communicate isn't working?

6. Jesus wants to heal our hearts - every scar, every heartbreak. Briefly share a time in your life when you experienced the healing power of Jesus.

JUST BETWEEN US

Marriage is two people that take turns being strong for each other in their weak moments. Each of you choose one area of your life that you want to receive healing. Share with each other that struggle and how you feel, pray together and trust God to bring healing.

SESSION SEVEN

NAKED & ALONE

For husbands, this means love your wives,
just as Christ loved the church
and gave himself up for her.

EPHESIANS 5:25 (NIV)

God calls us to love each other the way He loves us. The happiest marriages have a husband and a wife who both understand this principle and do their best to live it out.

We must commit to be unified with our spouses no matter how we are feeling. When both the husband and the wife make it their mission to serve one another, their hearts are going to be filled up in the process, and their marriage will thrive.

Your marriage is never going to work when it's all about you. Let go of your pride and your way. Marriage is about becoming one.

"Prayer is powerful, and it always brings results. Sometimes God uses prayer to change our circumstances, and sometimes He uses prayer to simply change our perspective about our circumstances." – Dave Willis, The Naked Marriage | Pg. 109

MARRIAGE MIRRORS
THE TYPE OF
RELATIONSHIP
GOD WANTS TO
HAVE WITH US: ONE
OF PARTNERSHIP,
FRIENDSHIP,
AND UNITY.

XO ▶ Watch "Session 7 - Naked & Alone" on XO Now.

DISCUSSION QUESTIONS

1. Do you feel like you and your spouse are close? Or do you feel that you have drifted apart?

2. Do you feel like your marriage is more often in the *loveseat* or the *me-seat*? Are you and your spouse in agreement on your view of where each thinks you are sitting?

3. How do you treat your spouse the way God treats them?

4. Think of a time you were in the loveseat with your spouse. How did this influence your marriage?

5. What is one practical way you can serve your spouse no matter how you are feeling?

6. What is the difference between a peacemaker and a peacekeeper?

JUST BETWEEN US

Find a loveseat or a couch, sit close and share one specific thing that your spouse can do that encourages you to want to be on the "loveseat" with them. No accusations, no counterattacks, no blaming, just share and work on sitting on the loveseat.

Pray for God to soften your heart and reveal any area of pride that may be keeping you in the "me" seat.

NAKED FORGIVENESS

*Love is patient, love is kind. It does not envy, it
does not boast, it is not proud. It does not dishonor
others, it is not self-seeking, it is not easily angered,
it keeps no record of wrongs.*

1 CORINTHIANS 13:4-5 (NIV)

Forgiveness means loving someone enough to pursue reconciliation instead of revenge when someone has wronged you. That's what God has done for us. He offers us forgiveness and freedom despite our sin.

Unrealistic views of marriage may cause bitterness or unforgiveness to take root in our hearts toward our spouse. Apologizing and extending forgiveness is essential to cultivating a healthy marriage.

Extending grace and love to our spouse is what *naked forgiveness* looks like. God can heal you and your marriage. He has blessings hidden in your broken pieces.

"Grace is the centerpiece of a healthy and thriving marriage. If a husband and wife keep score in the marriage or hold a grudge, they both lose." – Ashley Willis, The Naked Marriage | Pg. 130

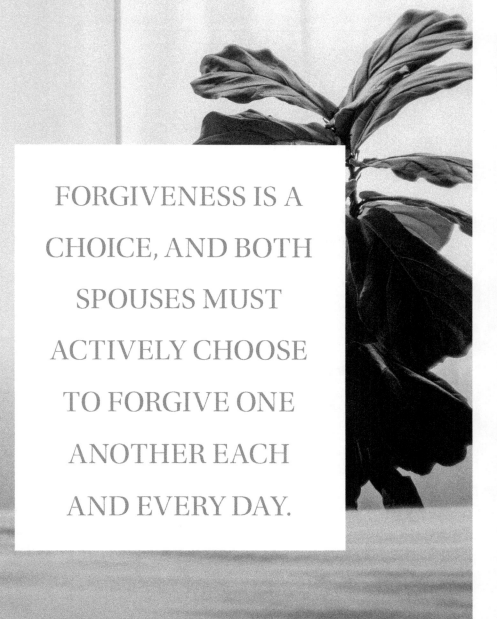

FORGIVENESS IS A CHOICE, AND BOTH SPOUSES MUST ACTIVELY CHOOSE TO FORGIVE ONE ANOTHER EACH AND EVERY DAY.

Watch "Session 8 - Naked Forgiveness" on XO Now.

DISCUSSION QUESTIONS

1.   What does forgiveness mean to you?

2.   How does "scorekeeping" affect your marriage?

3.   How would your marriage be different if you approach everything from the viewpoint of being on the same team?

4.   What's the difference between forgiveness and trust?

5.   What are ways to rebuild trust? How does one become trustworthy?

6.   Has your spouse asked for forgiveness and though you say you have forgiven, have you really let it go? What does the process of letting it go look like?

JUST BETWEEN US

Make this commitment, say it out loud and sign your names to it in this book: "I commit to forgive early and often, to not hold grudges and to extend the grace to you that was given me when God forgave me."

Take a look at yourself, is there something you're having a hard time forgiving or letting go of? In your prayer time, ask God to help you forgive your spouse and stop making them pay for something they've already asked forgiveness for.

NAKED PURPOSE

Then God blessed them and said, "Be fruitful and multiply. Fill the earth and govern it.

GENESIS 1:28a (NLT)

God has a masterful purpose for our marriages. Marriage is an amazing opportunity for husbands and wives to leave an eternal impact on those around them.

Serving creates an antidote to the toxicity of complacency in marriage. When a couple chooses to serve each other and the people around them, the marriage instantly improves. Evaluating where we are, setting a vision of where we want to be, and weeding out unproductive busyness is essential to knowing what are the best things to give our time and attention.

As we love one another, and together love others through our actions, then the world is changed. And ultimately, we are changed.

"When we choose to love and encourage our spouse the way Jesus loves them, our marriage will change. Don't treat your spouse the way they treat you; treat them the way God treats you." – Ashley Willis, The Naked Marriage | Pg. 146

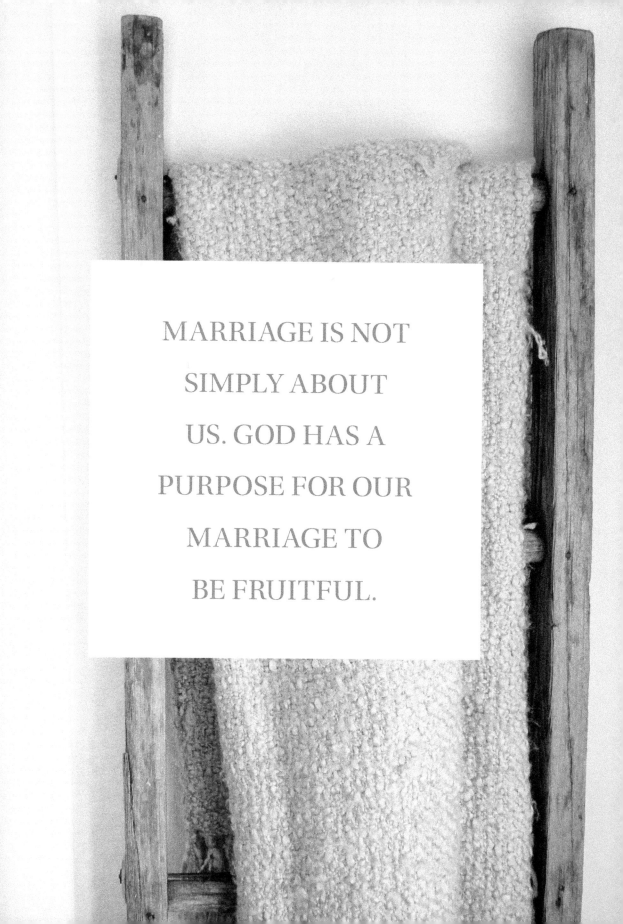

MARRIAGE IS NOT
SIMPLY ABOUT
US. GOD HAS A
PURPOSE FOR OUR
MARRIAGE TO
BE FRUITFUL.

Watch "Session 9 - Naked Purpose" on XO Now.

DISCUSSION QUESTIONS

1. What do you think a fruitful marriage looks like?

2. How does the weed of busyness choke out the healthy growth in your marriage? How do you recognize it, and what do you do to prune it out?

3. How do you stay rooted in Christ?

4. What do you think God is trying to prune from your life in this season?

5. We are not commissioned to prune each other, but we are responsible to prune our schedules. How do you decide what stays in your lives and what goes?

6. What is one area of your life that you feel is the most fruitful? The least fruitful? Why?

JUST BETWEEN US

Together, write down a list of the things that are most important for your family. (Ex: Serving, Church, Kids, Sports, Community, etc) Now talk about what two or three things that need to be cut out from your schedule to be able to give 100% to what you value most.

NAKED FOREVER

And let us run with endurance the race God has set before us. We do this by keeping our eyes on Jesus, the champion who initiates and perfects our faith.

HEBREWS 12:1-2 (NLT)

It's a good thing for couples to want to leave a legacy together. When we are legacy-minded it causes us to be fruitful, which influences others to want to be fruitful as well.

As a couple, you influence others to bear fruit by serving in partnership with your spouse to make the world a better place.

You and your spouse are unique and special. Together there are some great things God has for you and a distinct influence and mission that He has given you. God brought you together for a *greater purpose.*

God shows us, through prayer, how He wants us to make an impact in this world for His glory.

"The legacy of love He is creating in and through your marriage is just getting started. Keep going until you reach the finish line!" – Dave Willis, The Naked Marriage | Pg. 155

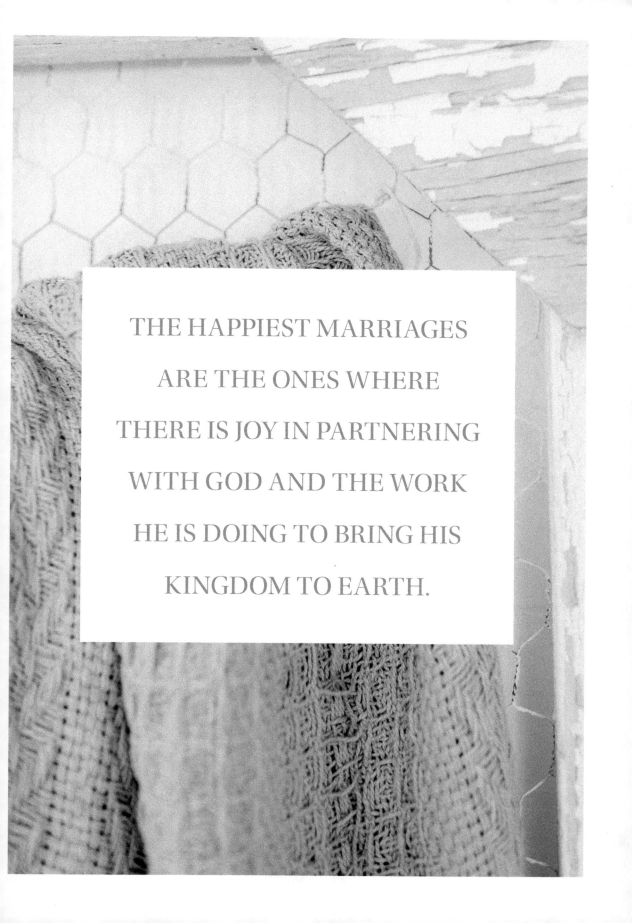

THE HAPPIEST MARRIAGES

ARE THE ONES WHERE

THERE IS JOY IN PARTNERING

WITH GOD AND THE WORK

HE IS DOING TO BRING HIS

KINGDOM TO EARTH.

Watch "Session 9 - Naked Purpose" on XO Now.

DISCUSSION QUESTIONS

1. Do you feel your family left you a legacy? If yes, what is it? Is it something you want to continue or something that needs to stop?

2. What legacy do you want to leave?

3. What do you think God has for you to do that will impact this world eternally?

4. How are you preparing for this future endeavor?

5. What are some gifts and talents that you and your spouse have that can be used to serve your church family and your community?

6. Investing in your spouse and your relationship with them is the foundation for your future legacy. What are you doing to invest in your marriage? Are you still dating?

JUST BETWEEN US

Plan a fun date night this week! It doesn't have to be expensive or elaborate. Set a regular weekly date night. Don't wait, do it right now!

Look for ways each week to invest in each other and make your relationship grow stronger. Your legacy begins with this investment.

Read a book together, go on dates, listen to a podcast, attend a marriage conference, have fun together, go on a walk, tell her how beautiful she is, tell him how much you love spending time with him, dance in the kitchen, do life together.

"You can have the close, thriving marriage that you long for. Keep on fighting for and investing in your marriage, and your connection will grow stronger!"

ASHLEY WILLIS

www.ingramcontent.com/pod-product-compliance
Lightning Source LLC
Jackson TN
JSHW071622070125
76711JS00018B/160